THE YOUNG LIFE OF MOTHER TERESA OF CALCUTTA

Claire Jordan Mohan

Illustrations

Jane Robbins

YOUNG SPARROW PRESS
P.O. Box 265 • Worcester, PA 19490
(215) 364-1945
(215) 997-0791

Mohan, Claire Jordan
    The Young Life of Mother Teresa of Calcutta

SUMMARY: Describes the young life of Mother Teresa as a child in
Yugoslavia. This account of her childhood and young womanhood is filled
with joyful experiences and the people and events in her life which led her
to be known throughout the world as a "living saint." Clearly written
factual story.

Young Sparrow Press, Box 265, Worcester, PA 19490
(215) 364-1945, (215) 997-0791.
Printed in the United States of America.
Fourth Printing
Cover art by Susannah Hart Thomer.
Cover design by Carrie Gamble.

ISBN #0-943135-25-7 $7.95 paperback
ISBN #0-943135-26-5 $14.95 hard cover

CONTENTS

The statue of the Madonna of Letnice.
The Bojaxhiu family made the pilgrimage
to the shrine in Letnice every year.

To Robin, Will, David, Katelyn, Heather, Kristen, Rose, Susannah, Sean, Robert, Ryan and Claire with the hope that all their paths will lead to God.

"Each person has a road to follow that is his own and he must follow that road."

— Missionaries in India

"God still loves the world through you and through me today. We must not be afraid to radiate God's love everywhere."

Mother Teresa
L'Osservatore Romano
April 8, 1991

1

A SURPRISING DAY

◆ ◆ ◆

"O clap your hands, all you people,
Shout to God with loud songs of joy."

Psalm 47

Has anyone ever asked you, "What will you be when you grow up?" It wouldn't surprise me if you've heard this question a hundred times by now — and given a hundred different replies. This story is about a little girl who found her answer when she was just about your age.

One sunny day in 1922 in the little town of Skopje (Sku-peeay), Yugoslavia, an amazing story began. The small church was crowded with young boys and girls quietly listening as the missionaries, home for a visit, told them of their adventures and challenges while serving God in far-away places. On that day, a seed was planted in the heart of one tiny dark-haired little girl who listened so carefully to them. When they were finished speaking, this little child left the group and walked thoughtfully up the hill to home, thinking of what she had just heard.

The sky was blue that day. Only a distant cloud floated over the river, just as her thoughts floated to the heavens above them. Her name was Gonxha Agnes Bojaxhiu (Gohn-ja Boy-ya-jee-oo). Someday far in the future, she would be called Mother Teresa, but she never dreamed of it then.

Walking alone with her secret dream, Gonxha felt the warm sun on the back of her neck. She wore her hair in a long braid and the heat she felt was like a blessing from God, giving her His love and speaking to her heart.

As she tripped up the hill toward her home, the leaves on the trees sang and there was joy in her heart. She began to hum a hymn that she had sung so often in the choir at church. The words filled her heart and soul. Her soft voice swelled as she lifted her head skyward, thinking of the missions, missionaries, and Jesus. At that moment, although she did not know it, God was calling her name. She was only twelve years old. She could not answer Him yet, but His voice would ring softly in her ears and, someday when she was older, she would hear the echo leading her on.

Gonxha was a pretty, loving girl with large brown eyes that seemed to take in everything around her. Her parents sensed a love of life in her. She was the baby of the family of three children. Aga, the older sister, was curly-haired and bright. She seemed always to be thinking of her studies. Her brother, Lazur, was straight and tall like his father. Although he was only two years older than she, already he was looking forward to serving his country in the army. Gonxha was playful and full of fun. She brought joy to the whole family. She could always make them smile.

Today, though smiling and happy as usual, her mother, whom the children called "Nana Loke" (mother of the soul), sensed there was something different about her. Gonxha walked slowly in the door and carefully hung her blue shawl on the nearby hook. As she took the orange her mother offered her, she seemed more grownup and serious than usual. Yet, there was a glow in her dark eyes that caused her mother to wonder.

"Well, my little one, what is on your mind?" her mother asked. "You look so thoughtful." Gonxha sat at the table close to her mother. "Nana," she replied, "today the missionaries came back from India. Our class listened to them for a long time. They told us of God's work in Calcutta and other places. You should have heard them. Oh, Nana, I wish I could go to India. I having a feeling inside that God wants me to go there someday."

Her mother reached out and held her. She loved her little girl so much. She loved the missions herself, but she was troubled at the thought of her little girl leaving her. They were a close and happy family. Silently, she wondered what God had in store for her child.

2

LOVING PARENTS

♦ ♦ ♦

"This is my commandment that you love one another as I have loved you."

John 15:12

Gonxha's mother, named Dronda, was a robust woman who wore her soft, wavy hair pulled back in a bun. She was a neat smiling lady who always seemed to be helping others. She was always taking local people in distress into their home, feeding them and caring for them even though she did not have much herself. She was always ready to share. Her three children, especially this youngest one, a mischievous, fun-loving tomboy, were always eager to lend a hand, too.

Just yesterday she had heard of a poor woman in their town who had a tumor and no one to care for her. As Dronda cooked their supper, she called to her children. "Come, let us get a place ready for Anja. She is poor and sick. We have plenty of room and we can care for her until she gets better." After hearing these words, they ran around their cozy home, plumping the pillows, freshening the linens, and making a comfortable place for the woman they had never met. Later they would go into town to bring her to their home. "Your mother is kind and good," she cried gratefully, "everyone loves her." And it was true. Because of her generous loving heart everyone did love her!

But on this curious day, Dronda just hugged her little daughter as she silently praised God. At the same time, her thoughts were of her dear husband, Nikola.

Gonxha's father, Nikola, had gone to heaven just three years before when she was nine years old. While he was alive they had had a very comfortable life. He was successful in his job and was generous to all. He distributed food and money to the poor. He taught his family to be compassionate. He would call his children to himself in the evening before bed and kneel with them as they said their prayers.

One night as he was tucking them in, he scolded Lazur, "Today you were selfish, my son." Turning to the others, he said, "My children, God has given you so much. You must always be good to others. Remember, my little ones, you must never take a morsel of food you are not prepared to share with others." These are words they always remembered.

Nikola was a strong intense man with dark burning eyes and heavy black hair. Gonxha was so proud of him. Until she was nine years old, the way of life had been different for this warm and loving family. Now their life seemed to flow around the church, the choir, and the needy. Then, it had revolved around their father and his dreams of country.

Every night their home would be filled with his friends — laughing, talking, planning. These men loved their country and yearned for it to be free. (Somehow the surrounding countries were always fighting for their little space. Even today, the tension goes on. Yugoslavia is divided and Skopje is now capital of Macedonia.)

3

A STRANGE NIGHT

◆ ◆ ◆

"Rejoice, even if for a little while you have to suffer trials."

I Peter 6

In the Bojaxhiu household, there was constant talk of the wonderful day of future independence. Sometimes, little Gonxha would sit on her tiny embroidered stool at her father's side, listening. Her face serious, she would ask him questions. "Someday, Honey, our country will be free," he would tell her. His arm would close around her and his eyes would shine brightly. "We must keep our language and traditions alive until that time comes." Gonxha did not quite understand, but with her brother and sister, she waited and worked and prayed for that day. In their hearts they knew their father would soon find the way.

Gonxha would often think, "I love my Papa so much and I love my country. I know everything will work out someday." She was just a little girl and could forget the problems of the world. So, she would dash out to the garden of their pretty home to pick flowers for her mother.

Those were happy and exciting days. Nikola was busy with his construction business and his meetings while Dronda spent her time caring for her children and her home. But it was soon to end. One night a strange thing happened. This night, when Gonxha was nine, her father came home from a political meeting. As they ran to him, he collapsed on the floor! Blood poured from his mouth! The children were frightened. "Oh, Papa," they cried tearfully, "what happened?" As the scared children looked at their father on the floor, they wondered, "Was he poisoned by his political enemies?"

They never knew for sure. Soon he was rushed to the hospital and the children fell to their knees before the crucifix. "Dear God," they begged, "please make our Papa well again." For hours they prayed as they clung together, waiting. When their mother came home, the night was still dark and she was weak and weary. She put her arms around them. "My children," she wept softly, "your Papa has gone to God."

It rained that night, long hard drops fell from the sky until morning, pounding on Gonxha's roof. For a long time she felt it would never stop raining in her heart. She felt a lump in her throat that wouldn't go away. She loved God, but she loved her Papa, too. Why did he have to go away?

Often she would sit sadly in the garden, wishing for him, yet knowing he wouldn't be there to pat her head or call his little girl to his side ever again.

4

LIFE WITHOUT PAPA

◆ ◆ ◆

"I can do all things through Christ who strengthens me."

Phillippians 4:13

Gonxha's bedroom was on the top of the house by the side of the river. The walls were white and the soft breeze always flowed in through the window. It was quiet and peaceful there. Her little room was like a nest, soft and serene, where she would fall asleep alone with her thoughts. It was a place to cry and a place to dream.

Eventually, Gonxha learned to live without her father and became accustomed to life with only her mother, brother, and sister. A tender, knowing mother would hold her close and talk to her about God's ways and her papa. "Someday, my little one, we will all be together again in Heaven," she'd say. Her mother's faith and love made days easier for the lonely little girl and soon she was her old self — more serious, but again happy and joyful.

At night when she was alone, her thoughts would roam far away from Skopje to a place called India — a strange but wonderful place where good men and women were doing God's work. She often read about this faraway country. She would picture the little children there and the love she would bring them. She would pray, "Jesus, I love you. Show me the way."

The days went swiftly by for this busy family. Dronda was gifted in embroidering, so she started a business to support them. And even though Nikola's political meetings were gone, the house was rarely empty. Their doors were always opening to the poor, sick, and homeless. "Let's share our supper tonight," they would hear their mother say. "I heard of someone who is hungry." Soon, others less fortunate would sit, smiling, enjoying their supper.

Every day, just before the Angelus bells would peal in the church steeple, Dronda would say to her children, "Let's hurry to church. Don't forget your rosary." It was not far, but sometimes they would race to see who could get there first. Other times they would walk slowly, holding on to their mother as she talked to them of God or of the flowers and birds they would see along the way.

With parents so full of ideals and love, it is no wonder that Gonxha should hear God's call. But still on that sunny day she was only twelve years old and did not suspect her future.

She could not even think of becoming a missionary sister, or ever leaving her dear mother, brother, and sister.

5

GROWING UP

◆ ◆ ◆

"Know that I am with you and will watch over you wherever you go."

Genesis 28:15

For the next six years, life was serene and happy. Gonxha's days were filled with music for she loved to sing both in church and in the town choir. God had blessed her with a beautiful voice and others would marvel as she sang alone. Sometimes, she would picture her Papa, safe with the Heavenly Father, listening to her. Then her voice would ring out all the sweeter. "Listen," people would say, "she has the voice of an angel!"

Following in the kindly footsteps of her mama and papa, she was always doing good. She coached her classmates after school, and spent many hours in church praying. Often letters from the missionaries would be read to the children and on her own Gonxha read many Catholic newspapers and magazines telling of the missions. Gonxha could not forget them.

One night at a church meeting when she was thirteen, the parish priest showed a map of the world.

Bright-eyed Gonxha amazed everyone by going up to the map and explaining the activities and exact location of every one of the missions. "She will serve the Lord herself someday," an old woman was heard to say. Even her pastor thought, "She is called by God."

When she was eighteen, these words came true. It was 1928 and a glorious day for their town. The missionaries had just come home. It was a time of celebration. Everyone wore their most colorful clothes. There was singing and music, as everyone welcomed them and gathered around to hear their stories.

Aga, who was now a milliner in town, heard the news first. Hurrying home, she exclaimed, "Gonxha, they are here!" And Gonxha, who had so often confided her dreams to her sister, knew it was the moment for which she had been waiting in her secret heart. Her mother cautioned her, "Wait a bit and think more about this, Gonxha." "No, Nana," she replied, "I must go. I have been thinking about this for six years."

Quickly, she put on her best dress, brushed her hair, and ran to meet the missionary sisters. She listened to their stories, then she was finally able to speak to one alone. "I want to serve God like you," she said shyly. "I know this is God's wish for me. I have known it since I was twelve years old."

Have you ever held a dream in your heart so long? Six years is a very long time in a child's life, as you know. Perhaps you remember yearning for a special toy and finally it was yours. If so, you will understand a little of what Gonxha felt that day.

Her waiting was over. Soon the Loreto sisters welcomed this young woman whom they saw so full of faith and love. "We will be so very happy to have you join us," they told her. "First, you must go to Ireland to prepare yourself, then you may join our missionaries in India." Gonxha thought her heart would burst!

6

A NEW BEGINNING

♦ ♦ ♦

"God is love and those who abide in love abide in God and God abides in them."

John 4:16

Days passed and soon it was time for Gonxha to leave. She boarded a train for the long trip. It took her to Paris, France. Then she had to sail on a ship to Ireland — a long trip for this shy young girl who had never been away from home.

As her family said good-bye, she felt elated, yet she was sad. This time, there were warm tears running down her cheeks. How could she leave these dear ones? As she hugged her mother tightly, only her love for God spurred her on. She wondered, "Will I ever see this dear mother again?"...And she never did! She started her long journey and it was years before she ever came home again and by that time her mama had been called by God.

Although her mother and Aga were happy for her, her brother Lazur was another story. He had left home six years before. He was a lieutenant in a military academy in Albania and was very proud of himself. When Gonxha wrote him of her commitment to God, he was very shocked at what she was doing. "How could you," he wrote, "a girl like you — so lively, so pretty, so hearty, become a nun? Do you realize that you are burying yourself?"

Gonxha felt far from buried. She felt alive and full of life. His letter made her angry and she replied, "You think you are so important, as an official serving the king of two million subjects. Well, I am an official, too, serving the King of the whole world. Which one of us is right?" When Lazur received her reply, he was startled at her reaction. He realized in time that she had made the better choice.

Gonxha studied very hard in Ireland where she learned to speak English. After six weeks, she was finally on her way to India. It was the culmination of all her hopes and dreams. Here at the novitiate she studied some more. She made her first promises to God (called vows by the sisters), and then six years later the final ones, meaning she would always stay true to God in religious life. Each day of all those years she spent time in prayer and teaching just as she had dreamed so long ago.

Sisters at that time chose new names as a sign that they were starting a new life with God. Gonxha chose the name "Teresa" after her favorite saint. She was now called Sister Teresa.

After two years of study, Sister Teresa had been sent

to Calcutta to teach history and geography at St. Mary's School. This was a place of quiet, beautiful gardens behind high walls. These walls hid the wretched scenes of poverty and slums on the other side from the eyes of the wealthy girls who were students there.

Sister Teresa was very happy. Although many times she was saddened by the poor who suffered so close to her, she loved her work. It would seem she would never want to leave. Her dream had come true and she was at peace.

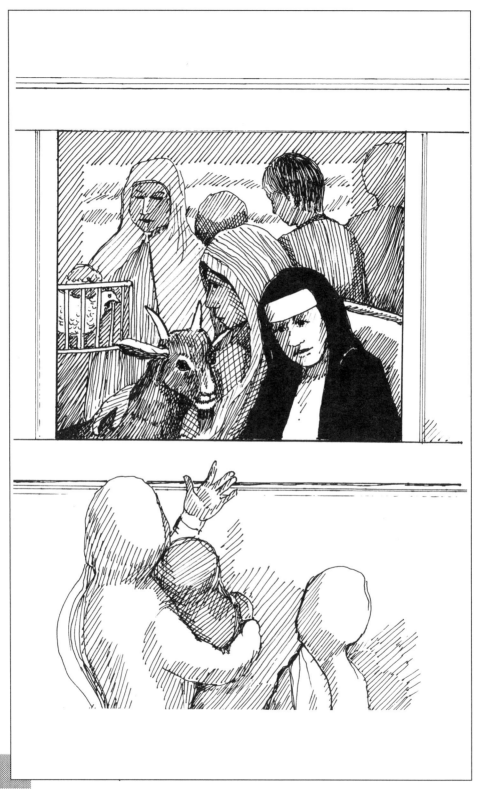

7

A BIG CHANGE

◆ ◆ ◆

"Peace be with you. As the Father has sent me, so I send you."

John 20:19

But we never know what God has in mind for us and Sister Teresa certainly did not. God had bigger plans for her. One day, a few years later, things changed. Her Superior told her, "Sister Teresa, you are to go to Darjeeling to make a retreat. You will take the early train tomorrow morning."

Nothing was unusual about that. Nuns make retreats every year. And it was just an ordinary train, its steam engine puffing it from town to town. Who would have thought it would change her life? Certainly not Sister Teresa as she carried her small bag and boarded the train with her ticket in her hand.

She seated herself near a window next to a man with a goat, thinking how fortunate she was to get a seat. Suddenly, she was totally conscious of the poor and miserable around her. They were everywhere — ragged and dirty men, women, and children. As she gazed out the window, she saw more sad-eyed beggars staring at the passengers. They called out, as their hollow eyes pleaded, but no one seemed to care.

The train shook as it slowly moved down the dusty track coming into Darjeeling, a hot and noisy city. Sister Teresa shook, too, in compassion and sadness. It was God speaking to her heart again. "You must leave the Convent of Loreto," He seemed to tell her, "your work there is done. Now, I want you to care for these sick and homeless, my most destitute people — for these are my children, too."

As she felt these words permeate her being, she knew no doubt. She could do anything God wanted with His help. "He will show me the way," she thought. And He did. Sister Teresa bowed her head in prayer. With that moment of decision, she knew she must leave the quiet convent walls and go into the terrible noisy streets herself. It would not be easy, yet, she would take God's peace and joy with her.

Now, nuns cannot simply go around changing their minds as you and I. They have made special promises to God that cannot be broken. Sister Teresa had promised to live her life inside convent walls. How could she leave now to live with the poor?

To do this, she had to get permission to change her way of life from the Archbishop of Calcutta. He wondered how she, a European in a sari, would be accepted by the Indian people. Then she had to speak to the Holy Father, the Pope in Rome, himself. But all things work in God's way. Soon permission was granted and Sister Teresa was free to follow God's plan for her, even though she herself was not totally sure what it might be.

There were serious problems to be worked out. Sister Teresa thought, "I am a school teacher, how can I help the sick?" Undaunted by this, she remembered the Sisters in Patna who were nurses and doctors. She went to them and asked, "Sisters, would you train me in medical work so that I can care for the sick and the poor?" Knowing the desperate need, they answered, "Of course, we will be happy to teach you."

Sister Teresa learned very quickly and soon was able to start the work she was called to do. Some days she visited the poor in their dark hovels and on the street, or tended the ill and crippled. Some days she would see little wandering beggar children. The teacher in her answered their call and she went to the slums to teach them, using dusty sidewalks as a blackboard.

8

MOTHER TERESA AT WORK

◆ ◆ ◆

"Whatsoever you do to the least of my brothers that you do unto me."

Matthew 25:40

What a seemingly hard beginning! How could one Sister do all this work? Was God asking too much? No, for while God had spoken to Sister Teresa's heart, He had also spoken to others. Soon two older girls from the school where she had taught, begged, "Sister Teresa, please let us work with you." They joined her and in time were followed by many others — doctors, nurses, and helpers.

When Sister Teresa started, she had only a few rupees and no place to care for these people, but high officials and wealthy people seeing her accomplishments and desire, found her rooms, gave her money, and all the other things she needed.

Today, an important part of the sisters' work is to pick up the dying from the streets. (In India, hundreds of thousands live their whole lives without a place to call home.)

One day Mother Teresa (as her helpers now called her) picked up a woman from the street who was half eaten by rats and ants. Distraught, she rushed to the hospital, saying, "Please give this woman medicine and a bed." To her shock and dismay, they said, "Take her away. We have too many sick here already. There is nothing we can do. Take her back to the corner to die."

That was the day, Mother Teresa started her home for the dying — a place for sick persons that hospitals turn away. She gives them a warm place to die where the sisters tend their wounds, clean their bodies, and most importantly, give them love.

Many years have passed since that moment. Every day Mother Teresa is finding new workers, new problems, and new places in need throughout the world. No one from the tiniest baby found in a trash can to the scorned leper is ever turned away. She will never say, "Sorry, there is no room." There is always room in the hearts of these special helpers of God. There is love and kindness for all.

Her special helpers, who come from all parts of the world, are called Sisters and Brothers of Charity. They dress simply — the women in white saris trimmed with blue, and the men in jeans and T-shirts. These good men and women have no possessions, but all are filled with love and kindness. Mother teaches them to have joy in their hearts and to always have a smile for everyone they meet.

Today, Mother Teresa's name and her work are known all over the entire world — not because she wanted, but because God wanted it. In spite of what her brother said, she is far from buried! Mother Teresa and her helpers are found among the poorest of the poor, living in poverty themselves, wherever they are needed. They are not only in India, but in many other countries, even the United States.

Everywhere she has gone, God has given her what she needed. In each of these suffering and lonely people she always sees Him. The little seed planted in Gonxha's heart in 1922 has become a living tree of life with branches flowing in all directions.

Mother Teresa is not young anymore, but she is still active and loving. Every day of her life is for God. The glow in her eyes is still shining like a flood light of love erasing the darkness of the world.

EPILOGUE

◆◆◆

"Serve the Lord with gladness."

Psalm 100:2

Gonxha Agnes Bojaxhiu, later known as Mother Teresa, was born on August 26, 1910 and baptized on August 27, in Skopje, Yugoslavia. Her parents were originally from peasant stock. However, her father was a successful contractor and a patriot.

She first felt God's call at twelve years of age and in 1928 at the age of eighteen, she joined the Loreto nuns. She went to Ireland to the Motherhouse of the Sisters of Loreto at Rathfarnum, Dublin, Ireland and then to India in 1929. There she taught geography at St. Mary's High School in Calcutta. She made her first vows in 1931 and her final vows in 1937. She later became principal of a school in Entally, a section of Calcutta not far from her present Motherhouse.

In 1948, while on a train traveling to make a retreat at Darjeeling, she experienced a second call, "a call within a call," as she described it. This time, she felt God's wish that she dedicate her life to the poor, sick, and homeless on the streets of India.

On April 12, 1948, Pope Pius XII granted her permission to start her Missionaries of Charity. She was soon joined by others. In 1950, she opened her Home for the Dying.

In 1965, she was joined by a group of men called Brothers who shared her work. Today, these Missionaries of Charity care for the dying, abandoned children, lepers, and the homeless poor, not only in India, but in Europe, North America, South America, and anywhere in the world where there is a need.

The Missionaries of Charity are in well over a hundred countries where they give wholehearted free service to the poorest of the poor in many places.

In addition to shelters for the homeless, there are AIDS homes in Spain, in Portugal, in Brazil, and in Honduras. In Africa and Haiti, there are homes for the sick. In the United States there are AIDS homes in New York; Washington, D.C.; Baltimore; Dallas; Atlanta; and San Francisco. There is an orphanage in Washington and soon there will be a home in China.

In 1979, she was awarded the Nobel Peace Prize. Her philosophy of life is encompassed in the words of Jesus, "Whatsoever you do to the least of my brethren that you do unto me."

Her sisters have no possessions other than their sari and a bucket to wash it in. They live the simple life of the poor they care for, and even when offered fine quarters, will not accept them.

GONXHA AGNES BOJAXHIU

Mother Teresa of Calcutta

August 26, 1910 – September 5, 1997

◆ ◆ ◆

On November 29, 1996, Mother Teresa told her doctors she wanted to go home. On September 5, 1997, God answered her prayer. He took her home, not to her convent here on earth, but to her true home in heaven with Him.

Mother Teresa once told her followers, "I have only one message of peace and that is to love one another as God loves each one of you. Jesus came to give us the good news that God loves us and that He wants us to love one another. And when the times comes to die and go home to God again, we will hear Him say, 'Come and possess the Kingdom I have prepared for you, because I was hungry and you gave me to eat, I was naked and you clothed me, I was sick and you visited me. Whatever you did to the least of my brethren, you did it to me.' "

We can be sure Mother Teresa, who lived her life caring for the needs of others, was warmly welcomed into God's kingdom.

Photo Credit: Robert S. Halvey, Photographer, Philadelphia, PA

CHRONOLOGY

◆ ◆ ◆

1910   Born on August 26

1919   Death of father

1922   First heard God's call at twelve years

1928   Met Loreto nuns at age eighteen

1928   Arrived in Dublin on November 29

1929   Started teaching at St. Mary's High
        School in Calcutta, India on January 18

1931   Made first vows on May 24

1937   Made final vows on May 24

1946   Heard "second call" on September 10

1948   Received permission to leave Loreto nuns
        on August 18

1950   Pope Pius XII approved the Order of the
        Missionaries of Charity

1952   Started Home for the Dying

1955   Opened first children's home –
        Sishu Bhauan

1957   Ministry included lepers

1965   Joined by Brothers of Charity

1971	Death of her mother at age eighty-three on July 12
1979	Awarded Nobel Peace Prize
1996	Has established homes, hospitals, and shelters all over the world
1997	Missionaries of Charity selected Sister Nirmala to succeed Mother Teresa as their leader
1997	Death of Mother Teresa at age eighty-seven on September 5

The following prayer of peace written by St. Francis of Assisi is the daily prayer of the Missionaries of Charity.

Lord, make me a channel of Thy peace that

Where there is hatred, I may bring love;

That where there is wrong, I may bring forgiveness;

That where there is discord, I may bring harmony;

That where there is error, I may bring truth;

That where there is doubt, I may bring faith;

That where there is despair, I may bring hope;

That where there are shadows, I may bring light;

That where there is sadness, I may bring joy.

Lord, grant that I may seek, rather to comfort than to be comforted, to understand than to be understood;

For it is in forgetting self that one finds;

It is in forgiving that one is forgiven;

It is by dying that one awakens to eternal life.

MOTHER TERESA SPEAKS

◆ ◆ ◆

The world would be a much better place if everyone smiled more. So smile, be cheerful, be joyous that God loves you.

We must do small things for one another with great love.

Each one of us is sent by God and his Church. Sent for what? Sent to be his love among men. Sent to bring his love and compassion to all.

Prayer gives us a clean heart and a clean heart can see God.

Let us not make a mistake — that hunger is only for a piece of bread. The hunger of today is much greater: for love — to be wanted, to be loved, to be cared for, to be somebody.

The cup of water you give to the sick, the way you lift a dying man, the way you feed a baby, the way you teach an ignorant child... the joy with which you smile at your own at home — all this is God's love in the world today.

If you are searching for God and do not know where to begin, learn to pray... You can pray anytime, anywhere. You do not have to be in a chapel or a church...We have to put our trust in Him. And if we pray, we will get the answers we need.

Pray and forgive.

There is only one God and He is God to all; therefore, it is important that everyone is seen as equal before God. I've always said we should help a Hindu become a better Hindu, a Muslim become a better Muslim, a Catholic become a better Catholic.

We are all capable of good and evil. We are not born bad; everyone has something good inside. Some hide it, some neglect it, but it is there. God created us to love and to be loved, so it is our test from God to choose one path or the other.

You must give what will cost you something. This, then, is giving not just what you can live without but what you can't live without or don't want to live without, something you really like... then your gift will have value before God. This giving is what I call love in action.

Remember that it is Christ who works through us — we are merely instruments for service.

It is not how much we do, but how much love we put into the doing.

ANYWAY

People are unreasonable, illogical, and self-centered,

Love them anyway.

If you do good, people will accuse you
of selfish, ulterior motives,

Do good anyway.

If you are successful
You win false friends and true enemies,

Succeed anyway.

The good you do will be forgotten tomorrow

Do good anyway.

Honesty and frankness make you vulnerable

Be honest and frank anyway.

What you spent years building
may be destroyed overnight,

Build anyway.

People really need help but may attack you
if you help them,

Help people anyway.

Give the world the best you have and
you may get kicked in the teeth,

Give the world the best you've got anyway.

*From a sign on the wall of Sishu Bhavan,
the children's home in Calcutta.*

SOME AWARDS FOR MOTHER TERESA
AND HER WORK

◆ ◆ ◆

1962   Padmachree ("Magnificant Lotus"), by the Indian Government

Magsaysay Award for International Understanding, Philippines

1971   Pope John XXIII Peace Prize, by Pope Paul VI

Good Samaritan Award, U.S.A.

John F. Kennedy International Award, U.S.A.

Honorary Doctor of Humane Letters, Catholic University of America

1972   Jawaharlal Nehru Award for International Understanding, by the Indian Government

1973   Templeton Award for Progress in Religion, Great Britain

1974   "Mater et Magistra" Award, by the Third Order of St. Francis of Assisi, U.S.A.

Honorary Doctorate, University of St. Francis Xavier, Canada

1975   FAO Ceres Medal, Rome

Albert Schweitzer Prize, U.S.A.

Twenty-fifth Anniversary Jubilee of the Missionaries of Charity celebrated in India, with honors from eighteen different religious denominations

1976   Honorary Doctorate, Santiniketan, India

1977   Honorary Doctor of Divinity, Cambridge University

1979   Balzan International Prize, Rome

Honorary Doctorate, Temple University, U.S.A.

Nobel Peace Prize, Oslo

1980   Bharat Ratna ("Jewel of India"), Indian Government

Mother Teresa has won these great international prizes, and many others, but none of this impresses her. She is happy only in that these awards often carry large cash stipends which she can use to bring happiness to the poor, sick, and lonely.

GLOSSARY

◆ ◆ ◆

abandoned – forsaken or deserted.

accolades – any award, honor or praising notice.

Archbishop – a bishop of highest rank.

brethren – brothers, fellow members of a congregation.

bun – hair gathered into a round coil or knot at the nape of the neck.

Calcutta – the capital of West Bengal state in East India.

compassionate – having or showing sympathy; pity.

convent – a community of nuns devoted to religious life under a superior.

crucifix – a cross with the figure of Jesus crucified on it.

culmination – to reach the highest point.

destitute – lacking food, clothing, and shelter.

dismay – to break down the courage of completely; to disillusion.

distraught – bewildered; deeply agitated.

embroidery – the art of working ornamental designs upon cloth with a needle and thread.

encompassed – surrounded; enveloped.

geography – the science dealing with the earth's surface as shown in arrangement of lands as well as climate, population, and land use.

hearty – warmhearted.

history – the study of past events.

holloweyed – empty; depressed.

hovel – a wretched hut.

hymn – a song in praise of God.

India – a republic in South Asia.

intense – earnest; strong feeling; serious.

leper – a person who has leprosy, a serious disease marked by destruction of tissue and loss of sensation.

lieutenant – commissioned officer in the military.

milliner – a person who creates or sells hats for women.

missionaries – people sent by a church to carry on religious or humanitarian work.

morsel – a small portion of food.

Nobel Peace Prize – award made each year for achievements and the promotion of peace.

novitiate – the period of study in a religious order.

patriot – one who loves, supports, and defends his country.

permeate – to pass through every part of.

philosophy – basic principles and concepts.

political – concerning seeking power in government.

rejoice – to feel joy or gladness.

retreat – a period spent in meditation and prayer.

robust – strong and healthy.

rosary – a string of beads on which Roman Catholic recite special prayers.

rupees – the basic unit of money of India, Nepal, and Pakistan.

sari – a garment consisting of a long cloth wrapped around the body with one end draped over one shoulder or head; worn by women chiefly in India.

Skopje – the capital of Macedonia in Southeast Yugoslavia.

Superior – the head of a convent.

supper – the evening meal.

tension – intense, suppressed suspension, anxiety, or excitement.

tumor – an abnormal swollen part on the body.

undaunted – not discouraged.

Yugoslavia – a republic on the Adriatic Sea.

EUROPE 1919-1938

Copyright by C.S. HAMMOND & CO., N.Y.

SCALE OF MILES

0 100 200 300 400 500

Boundaries as of March 1, 1938

Yugoslavia from the mid-1940's to 1991. Yugoslavia became a federal state with six republics in 1946. The country broke up in 1991 and now consists only of Serbia and Montenegro The four break-away republics ▬ declared independence.

WORLD BOOK map

INDEX

◆ ◆ ◆

FURTHER READINGS

◆ ◆ ◆

González-Balado, José Luis. *Mother Teresa in My Own Words.* Ligouri Publications, Ligouri, Missouri, 1996.

LeJoy, Edward. *We Do It For Jesus: Mother Teresa and Her Missionaries of Charity.* Oxford University Press, New York, 1977.

LeJoy, Edward. *A Woman in Love: Mother Teresa.* Ave Maria Press, Indiana, 1993.

Muggeridge, Malcolm. *Something Beautiful for God.* Harper & Row, New York, 1971.

Pepper, Curtis Bill. *I'm a Little Pencil in God's Hand.* McCalls Magazine, March 1980, pp. 73-83.

Porter, David. *Mother Teresa, the Early Years.* William B. Eerdmans Publishing Co., Grand Rapids, Michigan, 1986.

Serrou, Robert. *Teresa of Calcutta.* McGraw Hill Book Co., New York, 1980

Varley, Lucinda. *Mother Teresa: A Simple Path.* Ballantine Books, New York, 1995.

ABOUT THE AUTHOR

◆ ◆ ◆

CLAIRE JORDAN MOHAN, formerly of King of Prussia and Lansdale, now resides in Chalfont, Pennsylvania with her husband, Robert. Having retired from full-time teaching at Visitation B.V.M. School in Trooper, PA, she spends her time writing, painting and traveling. She is a CCD teacher at her parish and a tutor at Graterford Prison.

She has had many articles published in magazines and newspapers and has appeared on national radio and television shows, including Mother Angelica Live, the 700 Club and CNBC. On a recent trip to Rome for the Beatification of Blessed Frances Siedliska, Claire Mohan presented a special edition of her book to Pope John Paul II. Her book *The Young Life of Pope John Paul II* is also in his special library.

She is the mother of five children and grandmother of twelve. Claire is a graduate of Little Flower High School and is a 1984 summa cum laude graduate of Villanova University where she was valedictorian of her class. She attended Chestnut Hill College for graduate studies. Claire Jordan Mohan welcomes interviews and speaking engagements.

ABOUT THE ILLUSTRATOR

◆ ◆ ◆

JANE ROBBINS' clean, sharp illustrations reflect her classical training. An art major in high school, she was awarded a scholarship to Moore College of Art. She studied at Philadelphia College of Art, and Fleisher's Memorial in Philadelphia, Baum School in Allentown, and Bishop University in Quebec. She taught painting at the YWCA in Philadelphia and has held private art classes in her Red Hill, Pennsylvania home. In addition to Claire Mohan's current book, Mrs. Robbins illustrated Mrs. Mohan's previous book *The Young Life of Pope John Paul II*, as well as *Redheads* and has written and illustrated articles for magazines. The winner of numerous awards, her work is in private collections throughout the United States and Canada.

OTHER BOOKS
by Claire Jordan Mohan

◆ ◆ ◆

A Red Rose for Frania

This children's book offers young readers a thoughtful endearing story of Frances Siedliska's joys and struggles on her pathway to sainthood.

This story demonstrates courage and perseverance as it describes Frania's poor health and obstacles in committing to religious life.

Kaze's True Home

This delightful story of the young life Maria Kaupas will inspire each child as young Casimira follows her star to attain "the impossible dream." "Kaze" as she was called, was neither wealthy nor did she enjoy the opportunities of the young people of today, but she loved God and was able to share her love with others.

The Young Life of Pope John Paul II

Young and old will enjoy this story which details the young life of Pope John Paul II while a boy in Poland. The way Karol Wojtyla handles the triumphs of his life will inspire children to emulate this courageous boy. They learn his life was just like theirs — a mixture of sadness and joy. They meet "a real boy" who shares their hobbies and interests and in the end, grows up to be a most respected religious and world leader.

Young Sparrow Press • Box 265 • Worcester, PA 19490

WHAT OTHERS ARE SAYING ABOUT
The Young Life of Mother Teresa

◆ ◆ ◆

"Another wonderful book! Claire has a gift for writing from the child's point of view." —*Yvonne Walther, Editor*

"The author is an excellent storyteller. She has humanized Mother Teresa making her a model to emulate rather than a distant heroine to admire. The reader realizes that Mother Teresa's strength lies on the fact that she established specific goals based upon her desire to serve God and accepted the fact that if her goals were acceptable to God, He would arrange for her to accomplish them." — *Eugene Donahue, Teacher*

"I loved this book!" —*Rose Mohan, 4th Grade Student*

"This book is charming. The material is suitable for our elementary school children and is a very refreshing look at the life of one of the 20th century's leading figures. The style and presentation is appealing. Most children will be attracted to this book because of the manner in which the story of Mother Teresa is told." —*Patricia Gallagher, Author*

"A sweet story of the childhood of the Nobel Peace Prize recipient, Mother Teresa, this simply told narration of a girl's clear call to serve God, touches the reader's heart." —*Marian Peck, Librarian*

"The author's brief account of Mother Teresa is refreshing for children. Our children need to know that God is still raising up genuine heroes and heroines for their imitation. This book affords them the opportunity to see in their mind's eye something beautiful being done for God which is fact not mere fiction." —*Monsignor Francis Clemins, Pastor*